LION OF THE SKY

HAIKU FOR ALL SEASONS

LAURA PURDIE SALAS

ILLUSTRATIONS BY
MERCÈ LÓPEZ

Ⓜ MILLBROOK PRESS / MINNEAPOLIS

For my editor, Carol Hinz

    She studies the form:

        questions . . . scrapes . . . chisels . . . shapes . . .

    Sculptor of stories

—L.P.S.

To my sisters, who have been there from my first steps

—M.L.

Text copyright © 2019 by Laura Purdie Salas
Illustrations copyright © 2019 by Mercè López

Millbrook Press
A division of Lerner Publishing Group, Inc.
241 First Avenue North
Minneapolis, MN 55401 USA

For reading levels and more information, look up this title at www.lernerbooks.com.

Designed by Lindsey Owens.
Main body text set in Sunshine 18/22. Typeface provided by Chank.
The illustrations in this book were created with acrylic on paper and finished digitally.

Library of Congress Cataloging-in-Publication Data

Names: Salas, Laura Purdie, author. | López, Mercè, 1979– illustrator.
Title: Lion of the sky : haiku for all seasons / Laura Purdie Salas ; Mercè López.
Description: Minneapolis : Millbrook Press, [2019].
Identifiers: LCCN 2018024416 (print) | LCCN 2018022618 (ebook) |
   ISBN 9781512498097 (lb : alk. paper) | ISBN 9781541543836 (eb pdf)
Subjects: LCSH: Children's poetry, American.
Classification: LCC PS3619.A4256 A6 2019 (ebook) | LCC PS3619.A4256 (print) |
   DDC 811/.6—dc23

LC record available at https://lccn.loc.gov/2018024416

Manufactured in the United States of America
1-43577-33358-7/30/2018

SPRING

I am a wind bird,

sky skipper, diamond dipper,

DANCING on your string

colorful flowers—

we sprout on stems of people,

bloom only in rain

twigs, sticks, mud, feathers—
I'm a closely woven home
for cheep-chirping chicks

shhh! here's my secret:

soft petals hide inside me

coming soon—a **BL**o**OM**

I'm a **WRIGGLING** tube,

    soft underground tunneler—

I fear early birds

in the still-damp air,

you sail leaf boats across me—

tiny sidewalk pond

SUMMER

my fluffy seeds **D R I F T**

tiny puffs lift in the breeze

and land . . . who knows where?

wicked whine with wings,
   that's me, buzzing in your ear—
closer . . . closer . . . ouch!

I'm towers and moat

molded with hands, cups, buckets—

MIGHTY! till high tide

I love summer fields—
  left field, right field, center field
I fly to them all!

fire in our bellies,
we **FLICKER-FLASH** in twilight—
rich meadow of stars

you gasp as I roar,

my mane **EXPLODING**, sizzling—

lion of the sky!

FALL

my first-day outfit
is fresh paint and polished floors—
here come my new friends!

I'm a yellow train,

CARRYING thoughts from your brain

to the waiting page

I'm red, delicious—

with a quick twist of your wrist,

I'm free from the tree

reward for raking:

a crispy crowd of loud crunch

when you JUMP in me

I perch on the porch,

spooky face frozen in place,

fire **BURNING** inside

I search under oaks
and gather tasty treasures—
winter is coming

we are knitted twins,
SOFT as kittens, warm as hugs,
waiting to hold hands

I'm cold confetti

falling from a crystal sky,

blanketing the town

I'm thin silver blades,
spinning circles, carving lines—
you and I, we **FLY!**

lie down in whiteness

kick and **SWISH** and wave your arms

give me winter wings

firelight from the past—
I wink in the frozen sky,
waiting for wishes

in fur coat and cave

I exhale white clouds of breath,

DREAM of sun . . . green . . . spring

ABOUT RIDDLE-KU

Do you love riddles? Me too!

In April 2014, during National Poetry Month, I combined riddles with haiku and mask poems. The result is what I call the riddle-ku. Its three lines contain five syllables, seven syllables, and five syllables, like an American haiku. Something nonhuman narrates or speaks the poem, making it a mask poem. And the reader tries to guess what the narrator is! Riddle-ku were so much fun that I wrote a whole book's worth!

Ready to try writing a riddle-ku?

First, pick a common object. Brainstorm how it sounds, tastes, feels, looks, and smells. What does it do? When and where do you find it? Now write your riddle-ku as if you *are* the object. Stick to the syllable count, and include several clues. Be sure to use "I" or "my" or "me" in your poem.

Next, share your riddle-ku. Do friends solve it too easily? Take out a clue word. Do they all get it wrong? Insert a stronger clue to the answer.

Here's one more riddle-ku for you:

I'm a vast jungle
to ladybugs and earthworms—
a backyard carpet

If you guessed *grass* or *yard* or *lawn*, you're right! Now it's your turn!

FURTHER READING

HAIKU

Crews, Nina. *Seeing into Tomorrow: Haiku by Richard Wright*. Minneapolis: Millbrook Press, 2018.

Raczka, Bob. *Guyku: A Year of Haiku for Boys*. Boston: Houghton Mifflin Books for Children, 2010.

Rosenberg, Sydell. *H Is for Haiku: A Treasury of Haiku from A to Z*. Oklahoma City: Penny Candy Books, 2018.

Walker, Sally M. *Earth Verse: Haiku from the Ground Up*. Somerville, MA: Candlewick, 2018.

RIDDLE POEMS

Dotlich, Rebecca Kai. *When Riddles Come Rumbling: Poems to Ponder*. Honesdale, PA: WordSong, 2013.

Lewis, J. Patrick. *Spot the Plot: A Riddle Book of Book Riddles*. San Francisco: Chronicle Books, 2009.

SEASONS

Hopkins, Lee Bennett, ed. *Sharing the Seasons: A Book of Poems*. New York: Margaret K. McElderry Books, 2010.

Janeczko, Paul, ed. *Firefly July: A Year of Very Short Poems*. Somerville, MA: Candlewick, 2014.

Salas, Laura Purdie. *Snowman – Cold = Puddle: Spring Equations*. Watertown, MA: Charlesbridge, 2019.

ANSWER KEY

SPRING	SUMMER	FALL	WINTER
kite	dandelion	school	mittens
umbrella	mosquito	pencil	snow
nest	sandcastle	apple	ice skates
flower bud	baseball	leaf pile	snow angel
earthworm	fireflies	jack-o'-lantern	star
puddle	fireworks	squirrel	snoozing bear